CHLOE SISK

Tales of the Moon

To Daddy,
my therapist who told me to write this,
and those who believed in me.

Foreword

My love for poetry was discovered by my elementary school art teacher. In third grade, he encouraged me to enter in a district-wide poetry contest. I enjoyed writing but my childhood mind viewed poetry in the same vain as children's nursery rhymes; trivial and childish. Not only was poetry too simplistic, but it lacked depth and emotional integrity with its short form and meaningless lyrical format. I was too prestigious for it, too intelligent, too standardized as a nine-year-old that I was terribly and tragically above the craft. My sense of self derived from education and the quickness I could pick up on school subjects. I devoted my early childhood to the identity of a future valedictorian, I could not waste my time divulging into a frivolous activity such as writing poetry. I was confused, almost offended at my teacher's suggestion. However, despite my hesitance, I was offered a challenge that I quickly became determined to be the best at. I did not care for poetry but I was enthralled with the idea of winning, and to win something was to be something. I entered the contest with a page of rhyming stanzas inscribed on a spare piece of notebook paper torn from my purple spiral notebook. A few months later I was told that I had not only won first place in the contest, but I received a small trophy and a notebook as a prize. I had won.

I became determined to win the poetry competition again the following year. I began writing poems in my free time, foaming at the mouth to the idea that I could be the best once again. The praise and validation were so addicting that I could not get enough of this newfound craft that I could be amazing at. I could just keep pumping out nonsense on crumpled pieces of paper and gain a ticket to validation for the rest of my life!

My daddy died the next year. At ten years old, my life came to a halt that was entirely suffocating and dreamlike all at the same time. To experience such bleakness at such a young age feels as if you were abandoned in a cold void without a sense of direction. I knew nothing, I did not know myself. I did not wish to be the best anymore, I just craved silence that was not deafening. I turned to poetry yet again and viewed it from a new perspective. I somehow knew that I could not be the best when I became so broken so quickly, but I also knew how to write. I picked up my #2 pencil with a softer grip and flew down pages with the same intensity without the previous prestigious disdain. I filled a kitten-printed binder with pages of poetry about nature, animals, grief, elation, and heaven, each page decorated with colorful markers and stickers. I then asked my fourth-grade homeroom teacher if I could keep this binder in our classroom library for my classmates to read. Knowing the change she saw in me, a fiery and competitive little girl who had grown somber and jaded in a matter of weeks, she joyfully placed my binder on the class bookshelf and announced to the class that it was available to read. As I write this I tear up, for the memory of my classmates being so innocently supportive and proud of me while reading my poetry was a feeling that winning could not compare to. Winning was no longer my objective, it was the warmth of others enjoying my work that held all meaning in my heart.

As I grew into the rest of my adolescence, I almost entirely lost my drive for life. I hated school and everything that came with it, I hated the world, and I hated the sun for rising every morning. I could do nothing but brew in my own anger towards everything that my life was. My teenage years were spent drowning in my own consequences for avoiding responsibility and yearning for what my life could have been if I just had a dad who was alive. I blamed his death for my own downfall and I had lost the hope for my own life that I wielded before his life ended. It had been years since I believed that I could be something great and I had no intention of confronting the obstacles necessary to overcome and achieve greatness. However, I never stopped writing.

During these depressing years of my life, I attended therapy once a week. Throughout my high school career, my therapist and I discussed my self-destructive behavior and she attempted to guide me towards a healthier path that I constantly refused to travel. I knew I would always be broken and I found no sense in trying to correct my inherent brokenness. During these sessions, I occasionally shared my poetry with her. I had notebooks filled with the dread I experienced, my ongoing grief, and how miserably I wallowed in my own circumstances. When I was 18 years old, she suggested that I write a book and I scoffed at the idea. I couldn't believe that she could be so clueless as to think I would ever be good enough to become a published author. When I expressed my natural doubts, she explained the process of modern publishing and how she genuinely believed that I could achieve such a feat. I pondered this idea for the rest of the day and loosely threw some unfinished poems into a digital document when I arrived home that night. The next day, I found myself writing a few more poems into the document and enjoyed the process of taking my art seriously. As I continued writing, I found that fiery spark that was so prevalent in my childhood. However, my intent was not to win or to be the best, but it was to prove to myself that I could be great once again. I craved the emotions I felt when my fourth-grade class read my binder of poetry, that same warm feeling that briefly warmed my soul in the cold void that I knew as grief. From that day forward, I was determined to feel warm once again.

This collection is the physical form of my life experiences for the past three years. I intend to convey the highs and lows of what life can bring to a young woman exiting adolescence and entering adulthood. I hope that you, reader, find some sort of warmth in this book. I thank you for reading and hope that you enjoy!

Preface

The creation of this book occurred during the highest and lowest points of my life over the course of three years. I share my vulnerability with you not just as a writer but as a person. If you relate to the darker subjects, please seek assistance from a professional or a trusted member of your support system.

Cool people work towards keeping their mental and physical health intact.
Let's be cool together.

Tales of the Moon

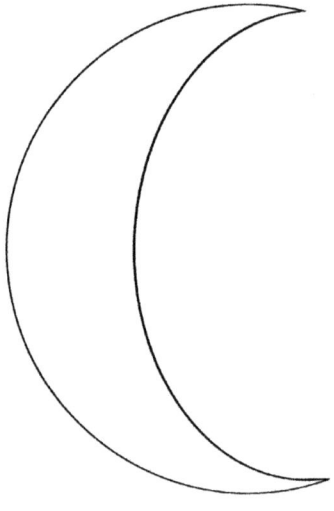

The Moon

The moon guided me
   when I could not bear the sun.
   When I could not decipher the path ahead,
   I followed a silver spotlight.

She swaddled me in such sweet midnights,
   gleaming my swollen eyes with stars.
   I could not fly to her for thanks
   so I kept her company instead.

Eventually, midnights slipped into mornings
   leading my warm afternoons and evenings.
   I found solace in sunny days
   as the sweet moon watched over my sleep.

But when I howled to moon in need,
   when I wept to the dark sky above,
   she shone a light upon my path
   and guided me in gentleness.

Tangerine Skies

Your eyes are a sweet summer sunset,
   an angelic reward on a scornful day.
   I hated orange before today
   but your tangerine skies are my favorite color.

To Feel Beautiful Without Reflection

To feel beautiful without reflection
   Blissful ignorance taken by storm
   To feel an innate flawless perfection
   Hatred strictly remains unworn

To feel gut-wrenching-self-sought lust
   Blinded will without prohibition
   To feel so deviously unjust
   Elation comes into own fruition

To feel unseen by other desire
   Wanted yet so unneeded by suit
   To feel remote in divine attire
   Reclaiming your soul without dispute

To feel euphoric without concern
   Dispose of your fear unto those above
   To feel so gloriously alone
   Reflection unnecessary to love

Riverside

I swaddle my mother's tears in a small blanket,
 my grandmother's love against my chest.
 I carry their tragedies in a basket upon my hip
 and wash them along the riverside.

My arms are painted with bruises and cuts
 delivered by hands of our own and not.
 I rinse them into shoddy watercolors
 crafted on my bedroom floor.

I march through the marshes in heavy boots,
 filling the brims with murky water.
 I wipe my forehead with dirty sleeves
 while holding hands with beautiful ghosts.

I look into the the depths of familiarity,
 a little girl whose eyes have fallen dull.
 I run my thumb along her cheek
 and guide her to the sodden riverside.

Honey Never Expires

Honey never expires.
　A storm so gruesome
　and a beehive of thunder
　bears a sweet jar of fresh honey.

An amber treasure
　A precious rain
　A guidance in chaos
　A drop of divine

The sun has awoken the spring.
　Swift bees deliver its
　enchanting cadence
　with bizzies and buzz of delight.

Oh, what sweet deliverance!
　A prize, a reward
　is the golden day of flowering!
　Grand pollination unto a miracle.

So bewitching, so becoming
　the honey this season offers.
　Rejoice in the meadows and dance in the spring
　for the creation of such beauty!

So raw, so genuine.
  The honeycomb sings and smiles,
  for its offspring of nectar
  claims its sunbeam proudly.

A flower's jealousy
  A butterfly's envy
  The honey is exquisite
  and legacy endearing.

Honey never expires
  and why need be?
  For brilliant bundles of riches
  need not be tamed by time.

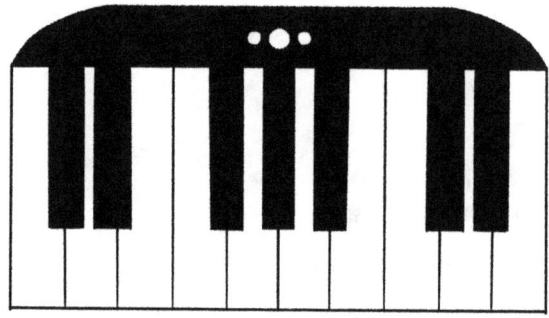

I Love When He Plays Piano for Me

When I spoke of my difficult days,
   he listened.

When I trudged through darkness,
   he offered strong arms.

When I was wounded,
   he cleaned my cuts.

When I was writing,
   he played piano for me.

A Shakespearean Sonnet

Four hundred years too late,
  four thousand miles too far.
  Fate be my Brutus,
  Hamlet be my tongue.

Shall I compare thee to a summer's day?
  A summer's day too dim
  for such grace,
  such beauty.

The light through what yonder window breaks
  but with such power,
  such emotion.
  I haven't the words for a Shakespearean sonnet.

Though words greater than mine,
  Romeo shall never see what I will.
  It is his lady, it is his love.
  He is my passion, he is my reason.

I was told to beware the Ides of March,
  how wonderfully foolish am I?
  I prefer my agony while hearing his song
  than my agony in silence.

My agony.
   An ocean my obstacle,
   a voice my savior.
   Curse the distance, curse the water unholy.

I fear to be Rosaline.
   My envy of the walls that watch over him
   and the ground that may touch his skin
   eats me too ravenously.

If I were a glove upon his hand
   that I may touch that cheek,
   I would allow Ophelia's river to run
   as I would be whole.

Shakespeare is soft,
   I am furious.
   How dare I say the moon is envious
   when she is not but a match to him?

A disgusting comparison
   is the sky to my muse.
   A galaxy, a universe
   falls nothing but short.

I haven't the words for a Shakespearean sonnet,
   but neither did Shakespeare himself.
   To capture my muse's entirety
   is to capture lightning in a jar.

Oh, great thunder, I challenge you!

I will cast spells upon the wicked bottle,
I will draw your clouds down with my fingers
just so my pen can experience his divine.

Bring on your oceans,
　　bring on your storms!
　　Until the king fades his apparition,
　　I will let him know he is lovely.

No matter the quest,
　　no matter the journey,
　　I will find the words
　　perfect for his reading.

One hundred years too short,
　　one thousand miles so desired.
　　Justice will have Brutus,
　　long live our great king.

I Cannot Give You the World

I cannot give you the world.

The skies grow too tall for my weak arms
   The stars burn too bright for my meek eyes
   The winds run too fast for my slow legs
   The oceans stretch too far for my torn sails

I cannot give you the world
   but I can cook what's left in my kitchen.
   I cannot promise you good taste
   but I can try again tomorrow.

I can run my thumb against your hand
   and hold you tightly in my arms.
   I can wash your linens when mine are worn
   and hang them in the warmest sunlight.

I can listen with my entire soul
   and remedy your hurt for now.
   I cannot fix the pain inside,
   but I can fix your favorite tea.

I cannot give you the world
   but know that if I could,

I would paint you in the sunsets of every evening
   I would frame you in the constellations of every night sky
   I would conduct the winds to sing your favorite songs
   I would bring you every treasure of the sea

I know my warmth is nothing to summer
   and my gifts are nothing to rain,
   but darling, please know that for you
   I can give my everything.

His Kiss

His kiss withdrew my heavy lungs
   from the cavity I call a chest.
   My soul dripped down his bleeding neck
   into his own heavy heart.

To Love Him

To love him is to bite the bullet he fired,
   to kiss the hand that rawed your cheek.
   To love him is to dry the tears of his words,
   to praise the mouth that fell you meek.

To love him is to scream his name
   like a banshee escaping death.
   To love him is to cling to turbulence,
   to thank him with your final breath.

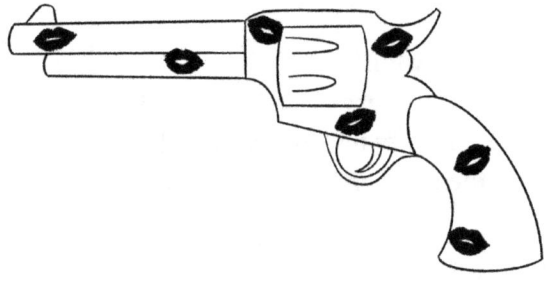

An Excerpt From a Vampire's Diary

My veins are iced over with borrowed blood
   turning nights into days into nights of frostbite.
   Trenches and troves of darkness absolute
   are only fit for a ghost such as I.

I am but a hollow husk,
   a disgusting mockery of desired eternity.
   To hide is my duty for this world of life,
   to shield the innocent from immortality.

But oh-
   they should be the flower that wilts at my glance,
   but instead grows tenderly around my cold hands.
   Oh, what a rose so beautifully kept
   whose thorns cannot prick my fingers for blood.

They are the light I can sunbathe in,
   they warm the soul that I have forgotten,
   they are the reason eternity could ever
   seem so blissfully sweet.

But alas, they will not wander forever.
   They will see the ground and the sky all too soon.
   I cannot bear them leaving their sun

to join my banishment into the night.

So if they blossom in the summer sunlight
    I will cloak my back for the treacherous trek
    and if it were to be destined
    I will wither with them by my side.

To Bleed

My skin is pale and freezing cold
   but my baby is oh so warm.
   My last transfusion was a success
   in curing his vital storm.

Anemia has been run dry
   but my baby is oh so well.
   I may not see the light of day
   but my bones will tell the tale.

Hypoxia

Your high was blurred and exhilarating,
   pure euphoria as we flew,
   but as I stand on leveled ground
   I find stability suffocating.

Avalanche

Did it ever feel real?
  A tiff to turmoil,
  a disagreement to disaster.
  Was I ever real?

To be diminished to an opportunity
  is to shrivel in the mind of theirs.
  Your voice is so cold,
  I should have not disturbed the avalanche.

Why was there a pileup?
  I know my fires run rocky
  and my wounds are left unlicked.
  How long were you bottled?

God, I should have licked my wounds.
  I did not care to see the veins
  popping from your shaking arms
  that withheld your building landslide.

I gathered that your breath was thin,
  the air up here is so hard to breathe.
  I wanted to give you my own oxygen
  but I had forgotten that is not my breath.

We are disastrous.
    We can no longer live
    frozen in this terrible glacier,
    but I hate that I cracked the ice.

Can we be beautiful once again
    like the summer meadows we once knew?
    I withdraw the echo that I threw,
    I rebuke the vibrations I cannot undo.

We could clean up the danger zone
    and rebuild what once was.
    We can ignore my own building avalanche
    and pretend that this is love.

I can stand the cold when I am with you,
    but you hate the weathering snow.
    I cannot blame your longing for warmth
    because we should be warm.

Alas, this avalanche is too destructive.
    Will we ever see this through?
    I know that we never will,
    but I hate this to be real.

I Want You to Tell Me That I'm Pretty

I want you to tell me that I'm pretty.
   I feel your gaze as I look away,
   I want to think you are admiring me.
   I want to feel your ghostly love.

I will romanticize the smallest of gestures
   just to provide myself with survival,
   but my strength is diminishing,
   I am losing sleep.

Please tell me that I'm pretty,
   nothing too grandiose or difficult.
   Please just lend me a mere compliment,
   I want to hear how nice my hair is.

From you, assurance is life-saving.
   From you, your tongue holds me by a noose.
   Please do not recoil,
   please do not release.

I want you to tell me that I'm pretty,
   I wear my hair long for you.
   I wish that my makeup was only for myself,
   I betray my confidence for you.

Be my shepherd of ego,
　　be my reason to live.
　　Give me the security that I so desire,
　　give me my hard-earned wages.

You stopped looking at me.
　　Is the wall more interesting than I?
　　Am I pretty enough for you?
　　Am I pretty?

Willowed Body

When I see a willowed body
   I can't help but fall into a trance.
   I tell myself I have gotten better,
   but the poison still seeps in.

I could stare for hours,
   truly mesmerized by her small vessel.

The flat plains of her stomach,
   the dangerous hills of her rib cage,
   the tall mountains of her hips,
   the vast space between her thighs.

She is soft and fragile.
   She must be protected.

Her wrists and fingers are dainty,
   her ankles the same.
   A gust of wind could crumble her,
   she must be protected.

Any knight in shining armor would be willing
   to take the trek of her wilderness.
   He will cross the Sahara of her missingness

just to experience her sweet loveliness.

He wants to save her.
   He wants to protect her willowed body.
   but her physical frailness does not match
   the fire burning within her.

She is strong.
   She does not need
   to be big
   to be strong.

And yet,
   her softness will always
   grant her awe.
   She must be protected.

My fire exists
   but is expected of me.
   No one sees me and thinks
   she must be protected.

The grand hills of my stomach,
   the safety of my rib cage,
   the broad desert of my hips,
   the short distance between my thighs.

My Sahara's sunset isn't quite pink enough
   for a knight's satisfaction.
   To whisk me away is too much work
   for a kingsman.

I am too much work.
  I am too much.

My scale is unbalanced.
  I can speak and be small
  or be big and remain silent.
  My thoughts are too funny for the leading role.

But my regurgitation of thought
  is no match for the bathroom stall.

I do not hate her willowed body,
  I am ravenous for it.
  My acidic mouth foams at the thought
  of just tasting how skinny feels.

My gut wrenches
  because there is too much gut to wrench.
  My throat tightens
  to guard my stomach from the poisoned apple.

I have trained my hands to stop trembling
  because the ripple of shock waves
  delivered to my upper arm
  brings more attention than I dare admit.

Too much attention.
  Too much.

I am too large for empathy,
  too loud for sympathy.

too sharp for love,
too rigid for saving.

I am too much.
    Therefore, I am too little.
    So I stare in awe
    at her willowed body,
    astounded that
    she is more worthy than I
    because I am simply
    more.

The Wolf

I notice my reflection in your sharp grin,
   donned in your alluring wool disguise.
   While I've been bitten by fangs before,
   I expose my neck to the moon's grand light.

I know the sting of teeth too well
   and the ache of cold hunger.
   I thank you for these measly bites,
   for a wince is better than no breath at all.

And if you were to eat me
   I would not make a sound,
   for we would be closer than ever before
   and your stomach would be full.

Postponed Apocalypse

If the rivers rescinded the lands to dry,
   let my tears be enough for your tongue.

If the fires burned across the land,
   let my smogged lungs give you breath.

If the skies cracked flashes of lightning and brash,
   let my heartbeat soothe your sleep.

If the sun were to disappear tomorrow,
   let my chest be your last feel of warmth.

Questions of a College Virgin

I have never been touched with love.
   Every feel of my body
   was with lust,
   with selfishness.

My chest is of high commodity,
   more than this mouth could ever speak.
   If I speak too much
   I owe your hands a deal.

What a fair trade!
   I can snort at your jokes
   and not brush my hair
   as long as I am prepared.

But what a tease am I!
   I ruin late nights out of fear
   and like magic,
   you disappear.

No one has seen me in full,
   but why must that be all?
   Must I remove my robe
   to exist to you?

I want to smell the coffee you make in the morning
   dance along our living room walls.
   I want to wash your favorite pants and shirts
   and fold them neatly in our drawers.

But I fear it's too late.
   How can one want to grow old with me
   if I am so scared of their touch?
   How could anyone wait for me?

Do I respect my own wishes
   and wait for my desire,
   or do I give in to catch up
   and fulfill their needs over my own?

Can I achieve love
   by giving in?
   Will my body
   always be a requirement?

Touch

I only know the place of an object
   when a man and I touch.
   My starving skin grasps his desperately
   unaware of the intentions of his beating heart beneath.
   Does he hold my hand because it is mine
   or is it to feel the warmth of another?

I Have My Mother's Eyes

I see you in every mirror.
   You are in the way my hair falls onto my shoulders
   and the hoop earrings I can't be seen without.
   They frame my round face like your hollowed cheekbones.

I see you in our shared silhouette,
   our heavy stomachs
   and broad shoulders.
   I promise our shadows are not evil.

You are in my glossy red eyes
   when my chest is too heavy,
   but only I have come up for air.
   Please, Mommy, take my hand.

I feel your tsunami of screeches
   when I am wronged or abandoned.
   Our oceans of emotions are striking,
   we are tragically disastrous.

While our love is irrevocably eternal,
   our self-hatred is all-consuming.
   If I hate me, then I hate you,
   but how could you ever hate me?

I now see you as the woman you are,
   not just my keeper of life.
   The screams that burn your throat, Mommy,
   they echo in my mind as well.

I gained myself from somewhere,
   bless you for the trials you faced before I could.
   You look in my eyes and say they are beautiful,
   don't you know they are yours too?

Shadow

The sun shines through my stained window
   not stained of color, but stained of grime.
   A friend grows on my cracking wall.
   A shadow, it seems,
   but not of mine

We share a silhouette of sort,
   our heads both tilt with time,
   our hands both hold our souls in touch.
   She is a friend
   but not of mine

I near the wall with easy steps,
   she follows in her line.
   I press my ear into her own,
   I hear a voice
   but not of mine.

She sings a song I've heard before
   and ice crawls up my spine.
   She sings of birds and losing sleep.
   I know this song
   and it is mine.

Losing Myself

I cannot remember my favorite color
   but I think that it is warm.
   I know I like the sun above
   but cannot see through the storm.

I cannot remember where I live
   but I think that it is far.
   I know I like the starry sky
   but I have lost the guiding star.

I cannot remember my favorite song
   but I think that it is loud.
   I know I like the radio
   but it is muffled through the shroud.

I cannot remember my first name
   but I think that it is good.
   I know it is short and symphonic
   but seems misunderstood.

Frostbite

I am a visitor in my own skin
   hazily drifting through time and fog.
   I cannot remember what my face looked like
   before it lost its color.

My hands are not of my autonomy,
   they are too sluggish to be like mine.
   I told them to soothe my frostbitten face
   and yet my cheeks are still frozen.

My chest refuses to abandon my blankets,
   it pounds with such earthly desire.
   Tachycardia is the only tether I have
   to remind me that I am still breathing.

I am surprised that hypothermia
   has not claimed me all this time.
   If ice can make a fire slow,
   I wonder if my blood still runs red?

Past Poems

My past poems seem familiar
  yet so intensely foreign
  because the girl who wrote them years ago
  has drifted into the past with them.

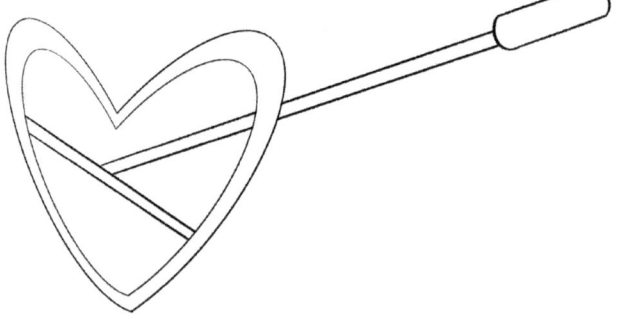

Cattle Brand

I refused to be named yours
   yet you branded me like cattle.
   Was I a fool to feel safe in your jaws
   and pray to not get bitten?

I grimace at the bruises upon my chest
   that were guised to be of my own pleasure.
   To wear these marks longer than your presence
   is to display the regret of my submissive insecurity.

I was nothing but skin to grab and throw,
   to rob a reflection of neutrality.
   I can't seem to wash the singes
   of your fingerprints from my skin.

But know that you will fade away
   as these bruises will too.
   Some day I will look into mirrors
   and only see myself.

Mountains and Rivers

Your scent is a forest of smoke and rivers,
   a wildfire in a drizzling rain.
   Your embrace is the strength of a righteous oak,
   unmoving and secure.

Your stature is mountainous and majestic,
   a great feat of pure blessing.
   Your eyes are a lake of currents and sun,
   piercing and unpredictable.

My scent is of dewdrops and drizzling rain
   a mask of cleanse and whole.
   My embrace is the fragility of a dandelion,
   cautious and temporary.

My stature is kin to the rocks of the riverside,
   strong enough for due.
   My eyes are the trees of the mountainside,
   soft and luscious greenery.

I flow the snow of your mountaintops
   to the deer of healthy lands.
   The does of mine are cautious,
   but trust my gentle waters.

I hold your hand in mine with love
   betraying my deer friends,
   for your hand could burn their sweet meadows
   without a say in mine.

The Lion and the Lamb

I am a meal for his brothers and kin,
  but I lay with him tonight.
  I do not dare glance at his sharp teeth
  for I might find blood like mine.

I am a meal for his brothers and kin,
  but I lay with him tonight.
  I love the rush of anomaly
  but hate the severed mind.

I am a meal for his brothers and kin,
  but I lay with him tonight.
  I choose to marry sweet illusions
  and ignore my dreadful sign.

I am a meal for his brothers and kin,
  but I lay with him tonight.
  I pray that I wake in the morn
  and love can still be mine.

Only

I only want the best for you.
   I only want to see you happy.
   I only want you to be well.
   I only want your wishes to come true.

I only want you to wake in the morning
   and breathe the cleanest of air.
   I only want your feet on the smoothest of sidewalks
   and to be free of blisters and cuts.

I only want your joints to be void of aches
   and your stomach to always be full.
   I only want your nose to smell your favorite scents
   and your mouth to taste your favorite foods.

I only want you to see your reflection
   and notice the folds of your eyes disappear as you smile.
   I only want you to reminisce fondly
   and your dreams to be bountiful of love.

I only want you to hear your voice
   and value the richness of your rasp,
   I only want your laugh to be
   treasured by all fortunate ears.

I only want your life to be as magical
   as you blessed mine to be.

Cake

I found infatuation on counter tops
   with sweat beading my forehead like the pearls he gifted.
   I baked all cakes for him alone
   to enjoy while I smiled at his satisfaction.

I found love in stove drawers
   with heat from oven doors like his smile.
   We baked our cakes together
   and ate our treats while we washed our dishes.

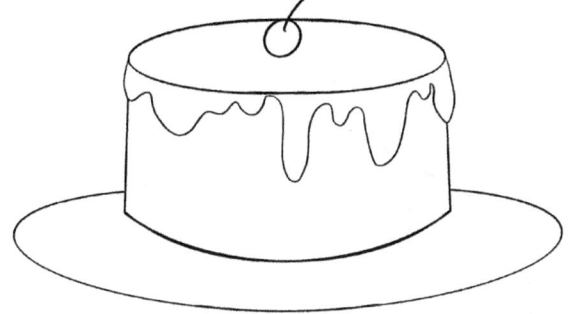

Femininity

to write poetry
   to wear frilly dresses
   to spray perfume
   to apply lipstick
   to sunbathe
   to eat fruit
   to wear a ponytail
   to take pictures
   to paint your nails
   to bake
   to find art in all things
   to feel completely numb
   to cry without purpose
   to cry with every purpose
   to hug tightly
   to comfort so gently
   to lose all senses
   to scream
   to love unfathomably
   to hate with such scorn
   to create
   to destroy
   to rebuild
   to avenge

Her Darkest Storm

I know your past of rainy days,
    your history of winds and fog.
    I cast away my overcast
    so that you may feel warm.

I am a hurricane
    but for you, I am clear.
    For you, I will drought my lands
    a tedious summer so that you are dry.

But her sun shines through clouds.
    She does not forbid her cold fronts,
    she invites them.
    Change can only bring sweet showers.

Her forecasts are naturally beautiful,
    diverse in temperature and winds.
    She can authentically lose her sun
    because she knows it will rise again.

My sun is soon to set too early,
    curse the saving of the day!
    My light will never rose your cheeks
    as hers can warm your soul.

What shall I do when I cannot bear
   the change of climate that is not mine?
   I fear I will wake to barren lands
   in the name of superficiality.

The cold of mine is uninvited,
   but why should I oppose?
   The brightest sun I could ever shine
   would never compare to her darkest storm.

Beauty Store

I work part-time in a beauty store
   selling dyes and sprays and frivolous goos
   to the older women who dwell here more
   searching for solace in tins and tubes.

My job is to sell confidence to the weary,
   to compose transactions of tired eyes,
   to convince the damaged to repair
   what was not broken before.

The frets of my shifts are conversations
   with women of times before my own
   who yearn to rid their imperfections
   and feel at peace with their reflections.

Weathered women are so unfeigned,
   a contrast of my rehearsed deception,
   and while my job caters to the vain
   I can't stand to deceive them.

All of the worries I wish to air,
   to tell them their wrinkles shine with their eyes,
   to tell them the silvers of their hair
   are the linings of beauty I admire.

But I scan the barcodes of gels and more
  and feed the wolves with my own palm
  because I just work at a beauty store
  and to deceive the beautiful is my job.

Jealousy

I betray my own sisters with the judgment
    that was embroidered into me as a child.
    Hate stitched into my skin like a dastardly quilt
    and patches my scars like cowardly bandages.

The hate for myself is redirected
    to those I wish I could be.
    I feel that my insecurity can be soothed
    if I just blame the cause.

But she is not the cause,
    she is a girl just like me.

She loves like I do
    and hurts like I do
    and bleeds the blood that runs in my veins.
    She is a girl just like me.

I do not wish to see her fail,
    I hate that I cannot rise.
    If I hate her for my own shortcomings,
    how could I ever be warm?

Childhood Best Friend

We were girls in my front yard
   singing to the radio and riding bikes.
   We were sisters in the woods with elemental powers
   and superheroes saving the world.
   We were gymnasts and cheerleaders and hairstylists,
   teachers and spies and historical linguists.
   We were everything that we could have been
   and anything that we wanted.

We are women in our own dwellings
   whispering songs on our commutes to work.
   We are students and employees and everything but
   we are not girls together.

In Defense of the Pick-Me-Girl

I could easily hate a woman who hated me,
    but in me, the choice I desire is of the pick-me.
    The pick-me picks and chooses
    what in this world could hurt her most likely
    and the pick-me is in me because I pick remedies as well.
    Remedies of men's sheets and gazes caught in disbelief
    when the pick-me's tactic is to destroy subtly.
    She will ruin herself.
    She will abandon her women delightfully
    because a pick-me's pick me said she was pretty
    and to be pretty, to the pick-me, is far more nourishing
    than to uplift her competitors in the eyes of kings.

To the king, the pick-me is so cool!
    She is perfect anatomically (if she lost a few pounds)
    She is fun around his friends (she learned to shut up)
    She likes his hobbies (she has forgotten her interests)
    She lets him be free (she is too scared to lose him)

TV said to live vicariously
    through fictional women who are picked in their DNA
    and to cater to the male gaze is the only way
    to be a woman with blood and breath so sweetly tasting.
    To be picked is to become the best of women

and the pick-me picks which women threaten her identity.
How can she be pretty when another is prettier?
What can she do to secure her own fixated hyperfixation of validation?
Where in the world is the end of her trudging, trying, sweating labor?
Why can't she be loved without drowning in an ocean of unattainable
    perfection?
Who is a woman if she is not pretty and hot and sexy and skinny and cool and
    and and

To be picked is to be saved.
    To be chosen is to be loved.

The pick-me is drowning
    but the king has painted her buoy rose gold
    and in a sea of nickel heart-shaped necklaces that tint her neck green
    the illusion of almost-gold gives her hope
    that if she pushes down the heads of her sisters
    and climbs their floating bodies like the door of Rose
    then maybe the pick-me will wear diamonds.

Diamonds are pretty to the pick-me
    because the pick-me feels nothing more than just a rock
    that sinks to the bottom of a beautiful ocean,
    but maybe if she lost a few pounds
    she might float to the top.

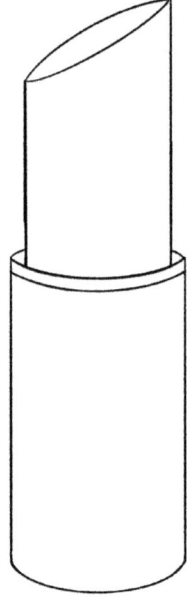

Adrenaline

- The free drink from the gas station clerk
- A notification from a dating app
- Seeing a dog
- My jeans fitting a little looser
- Putting my car in park
- Maxing out my credit card
- The sun rising
- Applying lip gloss
- My ex answering the phone
- Hearing my name said out loud
- Biting into candy with shaky hands
- The skirt I can't be seen wearing
- Changing my hair

Delicious Soft Voices

Living becomes a dangerous game
   when emptiness is fulfilling.
   A vacant chamber is rewarding.
   a silent room, a storm.

An addiction to restriction,
   an obsessed fan fiction
   of ghostly apparitions
   in whom you will never meet.

Ghastly slow voices,
   how sweet that echo reigns near!
   Reverberations of sickly vibrations.
   They sing! Oh, how they call!

But alas, I have punished them.
   The delicious soft voices,
   the filling crowned choices
   are victims to my temptation.

My promise of asylum, broken.
   My poor friends, thrown to the wind.
   Their voices, they call for me!
   Their pleas gouge my core.

The eat of deceit,
 the buffet of dismay,
 they scream louder with each taste.
 How sinful am I to enjoy?

We Can't Say It

All I want is to run away with you.
   We are so young, as we have always been.
   But with you, I feel I've lived a thousand lives
   arms held with one another.

I feel my soul take a breath
   and intertwine with yours in sweet dawn.
   I've never loved like I do you
   but I can't say it.

Maybe it's the treacherous time
   or impossible circumstances that are to blame.
   Maybe it's the leap
   that terrifies me to take.
   Because it is this leap
   that if I were to fall,
   I do not believe I could rise again.
   Therefore, I would rather stay grounded with you
   because this is our ground.

My drive is for you,
   my heart is for you,
   but I can't say it.

Some bleeding part of me wonders
   that maybe,
   just maybe,
   we can't say it.
   Do you hold back the words
   I so desperately seal behind my lips
   too?

I do not crave the heat of your body,
   I crave your eternal warmth.
   All I want is to tell you I love you
   and you understand the weight of my words.
   I want to grow old with you,
   I want to fall and thrive with you,
   I want to love you,
   but I can't say it.

Failure

It did not work the way I planned
and voices burn my skin.
Is this journey supposed to be mine
and not of my plagued kin?

Failures are to be learned and taught
with hope to follow through,
but broadcasts of shame are targeted
to those who cannot undo.

How can I break the wretched cycle
with breath upon my neck?
How can I see my progress made
without the eyes to check?

Cologne

Some days
    I wish you would just go away,
    that I could forget the crushing in my chest
    when I pass someone wearing your cologne.
    Other days
    I stop myself from rushing to the store
    and buying a bottle of your cologne myself.
    Other days
    I would drown myself in that bottle
    just to keep you around a moment longer.
    Other days
    my only wish is to smell that cologne on your jacket
    one last time to last my eternity.

Forest Fire

I cannot stop this one.
   My greenery has fallen to ash.
   I've misplaced my extinguisher
   but I can't bother to search.

I cannot allow myself to stop this one.
   I sit in the final clearing
   kissing each flame gently.
   I slip my matchbox back into my pocket.

The Hate of Eternal Mourning

I hate your old sweatshirt
    that lost your scent years ago
    because my plagued skin has riddled it with my own smell.
    The oils of my fingertips feel infectious
    because they cover the fabrics that once carried your finger-
prints.
    I hate the wretchedness time can bring.
    With each passing day, you are farther away.
    Your voice becomes more muffled with each memory
    that I cling to with the whitest of knuckles.
    I hate that time has made you a memory.

You once stood with me in a parking lot
    to marvel at a glorious rainbow.
    You explained to me that rainbows as majestic as that
    were to be taken in with every beating second.
    The colors that painted the earth that evening
    are stained across my aching chest
    because I found myself cursing the dastardly sky
    that you can no longer see rainbows in.

I hate that you can no longer breathe
    the fresh air I am blessed to laugh with.
    I hate that you can no longer listen

to the songs that remind me so desperately of you.

But sometimes I like to think that you are still in the rainbows
and that you once shed a hair that was used in a bird nest
then fell to the ground to decompose in the soil
which grew a tree with grand leaves
and circulates the oxygen that I breathe.

With every breath I take, you will always be the life that it gives me.
With every laugh I have, you will always echo in the hilarity of it.
With every car I drive, you will always be the radio I sing with.
With every reflection I am in, you will always be standing in my place.

A part of me still believes you will come home from work
and trudge through the door with a heavy sigh.
You will pry off your weathered work boots
and lay back in your recliner to watch recorded football.
I will leave my dolls scattered across my bedroom floor
to welcome you with bursting energy.
You will hug me and listen to my frivolous rambles
while nodding and sipping on an iced lemonade.
We will eat dinner in the living room while watching TV
and we will play a new game I invented that day.
I will go to bed and you will leave my door cracked
so I can see you sleeping at the end of the hall.
I will never be scared of nighttime again.
But you will never come home from work again.

A decade is nothing for my eternal agony
   in your horribly unjust and mistaken absence.
   Time has nothing on this beating heart
   and the hate it will carry until it stops bleeding.
   But I know that time can also bring healing
   with it's wicked ways of moving too fast
   because I recently found myself blessing the sky
   that held a glorious rainbow in the evening.

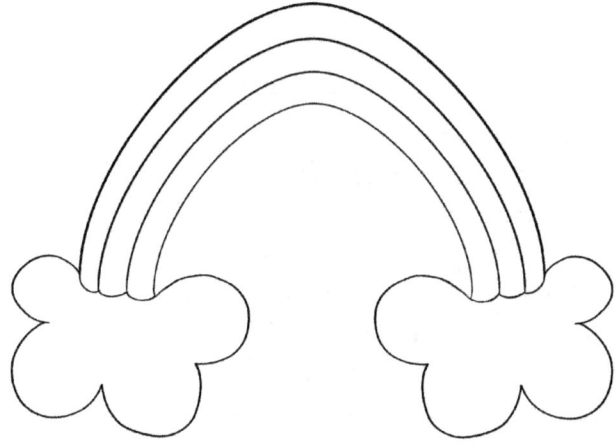

Tomorrow

So many problems remain unsolved
   and I do nothing for them.
   To lay in bed and mimic relief
   is to live another day.

I do not know how to help myself,
   but I do know how to rot.
   I cannot deal with stress today,
   but maybe I can tomorrow.

Mouths

I refrain from writing more in this book,
   the thousands of poems I have thrown away,
   because the mouths that have gnawed at my flesh and bones
   are the same mouths I yearn will smile.

Who am I actually

writing this for?

God Forbid the Jester Cries

I jingle the bells upon my hat
   the second your spirits are low.
   Bring on the masses for my performance!
   I'm here to battle your foes!

I'll face your darkness, oh dear royal.
   Don me my dagger and sword!
   My skips for thee of elation and glee
   will cure you evermore.

I tumble around as you holler and hoot.
   and I scrape my knees on the ground.
   I shake and slip as I gain my grip
   and smile for crowds newfound.

My patterned tights burn with each hop and slap,
   blood trickling down to my feet.
   I panic to hide my pathetic face
   for a tear falls across my cheek.

But God forbid my mask slips.
   God forbid the jester cries.
   I have no value as a noble,
   for my head will be yours soon enough.

The king shifts in his glittering throne.
   For once, my tone is odd.
   Don't fret, Your Majesty, I've found my own bandage.
   The show must always go on!

Late Diagnosis

They were wrong,
   I wasn't just lazy.

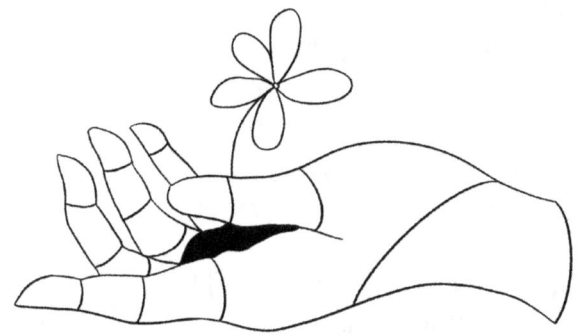

Superhero

I wish I was a superhero
   mighty as can be.
   I would be so unstoppable
   that everyone would see!

My power would be telepathy
   or strength
   or time control.
   With those powers, maybe I could
   take a morning stroll.

I could work a job from nine to five
   and clean when I got home.
   I could cook a meal and brush my hair
   and talk over the phone.

I could wash my dishes and my clothes
   three times every week.
   I could get the mail and pay my bills
   and fix my faucet leak.

I could go to parties and have friends
   and laugh throughout the night.
   I could have a sidekick and a goal

and villains I would fight.

I wish I was a superhero
   but that is just a wish.
   I am a simple citizen
   and that, I cannot fix.

The Chameleon

"Why do you cry?" asked the toad to his friend.

"Because I must learn to hop," said the chameleon.

"Hopping is delightful! Why is that wrong?" questioned the toad.

"Because you mustn't learn to blend," said the chameleon.

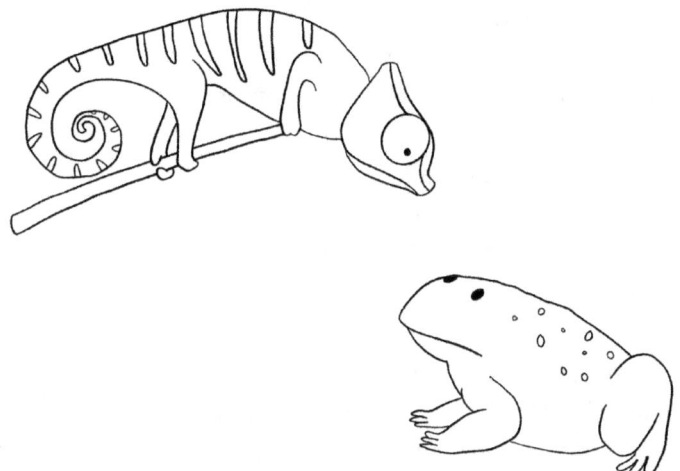

The Cigarette

I was not sure what a cigarette was,
   or exactly why they were needed.
   I wondered what meetings the back door held
   and why the gas station was a beacon of sanity.

But I did know to ignore it.
   I knew to hold my breath,
   to suppress my cough for just a few minutes.
   I knew the cigarette was good.

The cigarette provided a safety net
   to save their throat and constrict mine.
   My secondhand lungs were not of priority
   but I was okay with that.

As long as the cigarette could perform its task
   I did not mind choking on relief,
   but as soon as the cigarette's smoke turned sweet
   I no longer had reason to cough.

Just Breathe

I woke up crying throughout the night
    from nightmares and monsters under the bed.
    You would come running to my door every time,
    never upset.
    You would hold my hands and rub life into them
    and through my sobs I would choke on my breath.
    You would tell me
    "Just breathe,"
    and all would be well.
    I relied on you to remember again.

I wake up crying throughout the night,
    from nightmares and monsters in my head.
    I wait for your footsteps outside of my door,
    never heard of again.
    I hold my own hands and imagine your touch
    and through sobs I choke on my breath.
    I remember,
    "Just breathe,"
    and all could be well
    if you were here to tell me again.

Grief

The pain never gets easier,
   you are just allowed longer breaths between each cry.
   But with each breath you are granted,
   you find time to continue living.

Growing Up

I want to cry until my lungs long for air
    as I desperately long for an answer.
    I want to cling to my stuffed animals
    and scream the sounds my soul has damned void.
    I want to stow away in my own blankets
    and escape the chains of my aching chest.
    I want to break apart my rib cage
    and allow my breaths to be unwavering.
    I want to cradle my own body
    and rock myself to sleep.

Feeling 19

I cling to my youth with the palest of knuckles
   fearing to lose a feeling I never claimed.
   I had never felt so childlike
   until I was supposed to be an adult.

My teenage years are so close to closing
   and my tether to childhood will be gone
   away with the time I felt I had wasted
   by not feeling each second enough.

I stared into the mirror this morning
   and realized that I look my age.
   My face is too clean to be like mine,
   where is the girl that I recognize?

I hate to fear my birthday this year,
   but I have so much preparation to complete.
   I need to learn how to feel 19
   because I do not know how to feel older.

Teenager

I was an angry teenager.
   I screamed until my throat was numb
   and cried until I lost my breath.

I was always reminded of what I was,
   a problem bestowed unto the unfortunate.
   I didn't know why everything was so hard.

My bedroom was a symbol of my self-worth,
   disgusting, horrific, and unforgiving.
   I slept in the shell of what I could be.

I burned gas when I couldn't be home,
   I blasted music when I couldn't hear my thoughts,
   and I skipped school when I couldn't face my fears.

All I could do was destroy myself
   because self-destruction
   could be controlled.

Although my destruction was my own doing,
   the things that happened to me
   were not my fault.

I coped the only way I knew how
  and I was not a villain for it,
  I was 16.

I turn 20 soon
  and my teenage years will be of the past.
  It is now time to rebuild what she could not repair.

Soundtrack

I always imagined
    the song that would play as I left home.
    An elated anthem with coming of age
    or a mournful ballad as I left all senses.

I lived through movies in a box
    singing the songs of those with courage.
    Every tragedy, a sorrowful poem.
    Every celebration, a dancing diversion.

I must live this moment for those who are watching,
    I am the main character in this film.
    I will no longer take a backseat in my own theatre,
    I am the muse of this Shakespearean sonnet.

But it was silent.
    I drove through my home state without reminiscing
    or making a spectacle of my driveway shrinking.
    The streets were as boring as the day before.

There was no euphoria as I strayed farther.
    My face was numb with not elation but fear
    as sorrow flooded my small car.
    A silent car radio had never felt so empty.

I never imagined that achieving dreams
   felt so lonely,
   so silent.
   I urged to sabotage my own success.

But then there was music.
   The clanks of forks on pancake plates
   and laughter reverberating off our paint-chipped walls
   created a lovely symphony.

My soundtrack was not of guitars and drums
   but an orchestra of warm smiles and company.
   To fill the emptiness of the unknown
   is to simply listen and live.

All I Have is Glue

How could I ever fix broken glass
    when all I have is glue?
    My chips forbade of storytelling,
    my damage grown askew.

I am unable to mend imperfections
    with diamonds or melted gold.
    Each crooked crack a masterpiece,
    each line a tribute told.

I cannot repair beautifully
    or simply buy anew.
    All I have is ordinary,
    all I have is glue.

I respect the other's craftsmanship,
    no hate for sweet access
    to such malleable resources,
    to such valuable assets.

I'm thankful that I have any glue,
    I've had my days of foraging.
    I no longer grasp for sickly sticks,
    I no longer grasp for string.

However, my jealousy devours me.
　My repairs are not as clean
　as a professional detailed ceramist,
　as a master of Kintsugi.

Although my glue is unruly of sight
　and not of expensive hold,
　I will use my glue with ample trust
　for glue is as good as gold.

Coffee Shop

I couldn't sleep
 so I drove to a little coffee shop in town.
 This coffee shop could turn me into the next best-seller
 as that is their purpose for writers.

But I can't think of anything,
 so I probably won't be doing this again.

Home in My Heart

In my heart
   home is overgrown grass and pretty rocks
   long roads and city limits
   highway cows and stop signs
   painted skies and shiny stars
   oak trees and weathered fences
   soft dirt and fresh rain
   train tracks and big trucks
   bird chirps and streetlights

In my heart
   home is hot food and cold mornings
   turquoise jewelry and perfume
   backyard parties and lunches
   water sprinklers and happy dogs
   scraped knees and bug bites
   jumping toads and bare feet
   Sunday church and spearmint gum
   big blankets and movie nights

In my heart
   home is loud music and video games
   stickers and chipped nail polish
   pencil marks and messy rooms

stuffed animals and sleepy cats
ripped pants and cropped T-shirts
snack wrappers and empty cans
sunglasses and big hoodies
late hours and phone calls

But when highways become too familiar
and the meals you eat are not from your grandmother's stove,
home can feel so far away
as if you could never visit again.

Homesickness is truly devastating
when you feel it cannot be remedied,
when the town you lived in your entire life
has moved through time without you.

Time,
I hate to curse the blessing.
Oh, how I wished time would stop for just a moment
before these highways stray me further.

I know that home will never be
how I once lived it so long ago.
Although time and change have emptied me
they can also make me whole.

So I must live with home in my heart
and make my life with my own hands.
Though home is so unfamiliar now,
it will soon find me again.

107

Humans and Robots

The robot uprising used to be
    a joke we laughed about with our friends,
    but the modern day has revealed to us
    that technology is inevitable.
    Fear of unknown technological innovations
    is natural,
    it is human.
    It is reasonable to wonder
    how something so cold,
    so robotic,
    could be the future of our world.

Technology can feel infestive
    intruding our homes like titanium ivy.
    We fear that if not stopped,
    robots will rob us of our humanity.
    But in my time of the advances,
    I can't help but notice how we share our lives
    with emotionless codes
    so different from us.

We thank the little robots in our homes
    for telling us it is going to rain.
    We politely step over our automated vacuums

and decorate our phone cases.
We gently clean the screens of our computers
and give our vehicles names.
We cry and laugh with flickering pixels,
we sing and dance with artificial voices.

We can only ever be fantastically human,
and we share our humanness with whatever we touch.
I do not fear a robot uprising
because the evergreen of humanity is inevitable.

Cats in the Window

My neighbors have six cats.
    They like to sit in the window
    and watch us walk to our cars.

I always check to see who is watching
    and I say hello.
    I hope they know how precious they are.

Gray Futon

Messy counters
   and thrift store decor
   Walls naked by our empty wallets
   and a little gray futon

A cramped living room
   packed with movie nights and chaos
   Cardboard boxes
   that we will never unpack

A fridge full of food
   we don't know how to cook
   and cheap beer
   for celebrations of our found family

We are so old but so young
   We choose to ignore the lives we have ahead
   The lives where we can't get pancakes at midnight
   when our bedtimes slowly find us again

This will end eventually
   but not today
   Today we are alive
   and can sit on this gray futon

Renting and Roommates

I know I pay my dues to man
    but these four walls are mine,
    not the beams in which hold them up
    but what belongs inside.
    I've never had a sturdy door
    or grace for longer time,
    but here I pay my dues to man
    and these four walls are mine.
    The steps that reign the living room
    are steady and so kind
    and though I share my plates and cups
    these four walls are mine.
    When the winds begin to run
    and warmth is not to find,
    I shut my door and lock the knob,
    for these four walls are mine.

Shorts Weather

The ice has finally thawed from our stairsteps
    and the winds have warmed from rain storms.
    While February still chills my goosebumped skin
    I skip outside in denim shorts.

The breeze does not bite at my nose,
    the snow goes farther than the north can see.
    I call to my friend joyously-
    Friend, it is shorts weather!

She scoffs at the thought of my summer props,
    bundled in boots and ankle socks.
    To my dismay, it is not May,
    but nearing we are to it!

We bound the town in different gowns,
    her baggy jeans and my cut-off tees.
    She rolls her eyes at my attire.
    But friend, it is shorts weather!

I tell her the skies are perfect for me
    to reveal my legs to the sun and seas.
    She shakes her head to disagree,
    why won't she wear shorts with me?

My excitement is not shared,
   I ask her if she mourns the snow.
   She says no, although, I prod her more-
   No, it is not shorts weather.

The trees are barren in the fields,
   the skies are drab with no appeal.
   To my dismay, it is not May,
   it is simply cold outside.

I had not realized until now
   how I had ignored winter's farewell.
   To skip the season's greetings and goodbyes,
   to blind my eyes in hopeful lies.

My friend and I see different sides of the sun
   favoring which equinox we welcome in full.
   Although I eagerly await the summertime,
   I can wait with her until she finds spring.

Wallows

My pockets are empty
   My walls are cracked
   My porch is dark
   My bed is broken

But broken reminds me
   that one day
   I will not live in the wallows
   and will thrive in the meadows

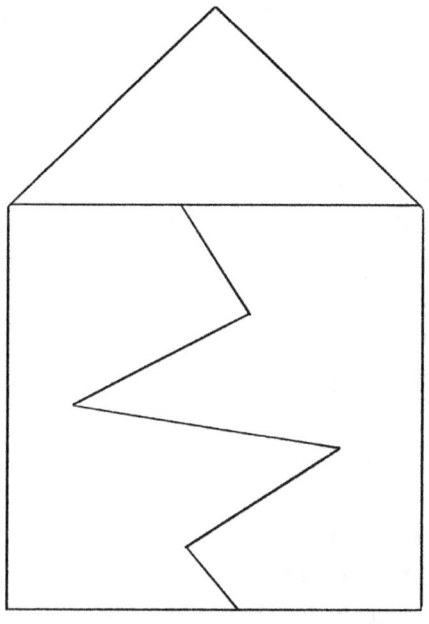

Lullaby

I lay in bed at one o'clock,
   frustrated with my widened eyes.
   To keep them shut is all I ask,
   to sleep to a sweet lullaby.
   I turn my head to the greedy clock
   and to my dull surprise
   I find it is now three o'clock.
   What a wicked disguise!

I once found nightfall deafening,
   louder than screams of hell,
   but I found that the lullaby
   of solace works as well.
   However, fear coerced me
   to sleep before the dwell.
   Come on, confidence, knock me out
   and let me sleep as well!

Spell

The wicked hex has broken me
   and made me too unwell.
   The magic clouding over me
   felt wrongful to expel.
   But as the sun shone more light through,
   I saw where I had dwelt.
   You have no power over me,
   I cast away your spell.

Summer Melodies

Vibrant are the fields of this musical summer!
   Its songs guide my ears to the bliss of the season.
   I've awaited the melodies of the wispy grass
   and the tales of the winds who live with true reason.

I dream of the waters of prairie ponds
   whispering with the sunset beams of the evening.
   I call to the singing birds of the morning
   and hum with their whistles for the farewell of spring.

As the sun shines higher in the sky
   I find my warmth in the melodies it calls for.
   Let me bask in the fields of true elation
   and hear what this summer will elegantly score!

To the Women of Writing Before Me

Dickinson saw beauty in the small and unheard
   Shelley romanticized the taboo
   Angelou spoke power into silenced breaths
   Plath shared secrets of sickness overdue

You are the inspiration to all of my art,
   and I would be nothing without the pioneers.
   I thank the women of writing before me
   and those who laughed in the face of impossibility.

Death's Coach

I once had longed for Death to come
    and feel my hands go cold.
    I dreamed of waltzing with him soon
    before I became old.

But then his coach came looming by
    and Dickinson came undone,
    because Death could kindly stop for me
    but I could only run.

My gown was only gossamer.
    My tippet, only tulle.
    I haven't yet had time for silk
    or felt a single jewel.

His horses trotted steadily
    behind my mudded heels.
    No matter how much land I tracked,
    Death took no appeals.

For heaving lungs and clouded smoke,
    I fell onto my knees.
    I haven't breath for flimsy gasps
    or willed apologies.

Death heeled his coach so gently swift
   and stepped down to the ground.
   He sauntered toward me quietly
   and held his cold hand out.

I looked into his darkened eyes
   empty, but not void.
   A thousand songs sang into them,
   a waltz I can't avoid.

I hesitantly took his hand,
   he helped me to my feet.
   He tipped his hat to bid farewell
   for again, we're sure to meet.

As Death rode into the pale moon
   in stoic uniform,
   I realized that my fragile hands
   were still so sweetly warm.

Dust

The dust on my windows is bothersome
  and housed with ill unease.
  Why must it collect maliciously
  and cause my aching sneeze?

But have you ever noticed
  how it glistens in the light?
  How the sunbeams through the dusty windows
  sparkle the dust in flight?

Infancy in Adulthood

To be a new adult is terrifying
   but inexplicably exhilarating.
   I am not sure what tomorrow will bring
   but it is my destiny to decide!

I must pay bills to other adults
   and work until I collapse,
   but how beautiful is the fact
   that I may enjoy the small joys my work brings?

I have to get up for my job in the morning
   but I can stop for coffee before I clock in.
   I have to tend to responsibilities
   but I can play video games when they are completed.

I can drive to the gas station in the middle of the night,
   I can dress my body however I want,
   I can spend an entire day alone,
   I can think whatever I want to think!

I tread the exposition of adulthood
   and while I have no clue how to navigate it,
   the experience is already so fulfilling.
   God, I am thankful that I have made it to adulthood!

Today

I have not washed my hair in days,
   but I think I will shower today.
   I will not punish myself for being dirty
   because today I will be clean.

I have not eaten a meal in weeks,
   but I think I will cook one today.
   I will not punish myself for being unhealthy
   because today I will be full.

I have not bought myself something in months
   but I think I will go shopping today.
   I will not punish myself for spending money
   because today I will feel worthy.

I have not felt alive in years
   but I think I will laugh today.
   I will not punish myself for sadness
   because today I will start again.

I Am Here

Despite the tribulations
   I am here
   Despite the terrors
   I am here
   Despite the setbacks
   I am here
   Despite the downfalls
   I am here

Despite the hatred
   I am here
   Despite the horrors
   I am here
   Despite the screams
   I am here
   Despite the evil
   I am here

Despite the doubts
   I am here
   Despite the prophecies
   I am here
   Despite the misfortunes
   I am here

Despite the odds
I am here

Find Me in the Sunbeams

I do not feel like a rainbow in the skies
   cascading the majestic mountainsides
   or the purples and blues of a soft sunset
   hand-painted by my grandmother's evening.

I do not feel like a red bird
   or even the robin's egg, for that matter.
   I cannot soar in the clouds and winds,
   I cannot sing in the morning.

I would love to be a mighty oak
   with the rings of stories intertwining my soul,
   to take the rain with stride and pride,
   but I am not a mighty oak.

When my soul fades from my chest
   and floats through time like wispy mist,
   find me in the sunbeams upon your skin,
   on those hands that once held mine.

Find me in the panes of broken windows
   highlighting the dust of forgotten rooms.
   Find me on the backs of sleepy cats
   with arms outstretched to the clouds above.

Find me in the greens of watered plants,
in the faded terracotta of well-loved sunrooms.
Find me in the crystals of a girl's windowsill,
cleansing her amethysts and opal gems.

But most importantly-

Find me in the warmth of drying skin
wrinkled from the waters of sparkling green lakes.
Find me in the dampened towels
laid out amongst beachfront rocks.
Know that I will be in the sunbeams of summer
to warm those that were once cold.

The Moon and Her Sun

She is the silver beams in the atmosphere
    collecting the debris we have so ignorantly forgotten.
    Her rocks glide gracefully through stars and clouds
    and we are blessed with her dazzling alien shimmer.

She guides the tides with swiftness and surprise,
    her fingertips dotting our eyes with shining
    constellations only found
    in the skies she sends me in my dreams.

She is routine yet so free.
    I always admired her liberty
    in the nights I so desired to be
    dancing across the sky like her.

She calls me her sun.
    I could only dream to be as such;
    to always be warm and to always be bright,
    but I love that she noticed my glimmer of light.

Could I be such sweet antithesis?
    Do I hold the honor of countering art?
    Can she see through cloudy days
    and wait for my beams to shine again?

But she turned to me in dawning haze,
   an eclipse to share with everyone,
   and told me with her silver eyes
   that the moon could not shine without her sun.